50 Summer Gourmet Dishes

By: Kelly Johnson

Table of Contents

- Lobster Roll
- Grilled Sea Bass
- Tuna Tartare
- Caprese Salad
- Grilled Asparagus with Hollandaise
- Shrimp Cocktail
- Summer Berry Salad
- Seared Scallops
- Gazpacho
- Lemon Herb Grilled Chicken
- Ceviche
- Roasted Corn with Chili Butter
- Burrata with Prosciutto
- Watermelon Feta Salad
- Grilled Lamb Chops
- Mahi-Mahi Tacos
- Lobster Bisque
- Grilled Octopus
- Heirloom Tomato Salad

- Avocado Toast with Poached Egg
- Zucchini Noodles with Pesto
- Grilled Swordfish
- Peach and Burrata Salad
- Crab Cakes
- Grilled Peach Salad
- Grilled Veggie Platter
- Beef Carpaccio
- Tomato Basil Bruschetta
- Smoked Salmon with Cucumber Salad
- Grilled Shrimp Skewers
- Grilled Chicken Caesar Salad
- Avocado and Shrimp Ceviche
- Stuffed Peppers with Quinoa
- Roasted Beet Salad with Goat Cheese
- Salmon Poke Bowl
- Roasted Vegetable Flatbread
- Lobster Mac and Cheese
- Grilled Fennel with Lemon
- Grilled Halloumi Cheese
- Grilled Fruit Salad

- Summer Risotto with Peas
- Poached Lobster Tail
- Fresh Tuna Sushi
- Watermelon Gazpacho
- Seared Ahi Tuna
- Grilled Eggplant with Feta
- Summer Squash Frittata
- Grilled Chicken and Peach Salad
- Shrimp and Grits
- Roasted Garlic and Herb Mussels

Lobster Roll

Ingredients:

- 2 lobster tails, cooked and chopped
- 2 tbsp mayonnaise
- 1 tbsp lemon juice
- 1 tbsp celery, finely chopped
- 1 tsp Dijon mustard
- Salt and pepper to taste
- 4 hot dog buns, lightly toasted
- Fresh parsley for garnish

Instructions:

1. Mix lobster meat with mayonnaise, lemon juice, celery, mustard, salt, and pepper.
2. Fill toasted buns with lobster mixture.
3. Garnish with fresh parsley and serve immediately.

Grilled Sea Bass

Ingredients:

- 2 sea bass fillets
- 2 tbsp olive oil
- 1 tbsp lemon juice
- 1 clove garlic, minced
- Salt and pepper to taste
- Fresh herbs for garnish (like parsley or thyme)

Instructions:

1. Preheat grill to medium-high heat.
2. Brush fish fillets with olive oil, lemon juice, garlic, salt, and pepper.
3. Grill for 3-4 minutes per side until the fish is cooked through and flakes easily.
4. Garnish with fresh herbs and serve.

Tuna Tartare

Ingredients:

- 1 lb fresh sushi-grade tuna, diced
- 1/4 cup soy sauce
- 1 tbsp sesame oil
- 1 tsp rice vinegar
- 1 tsp grated ginger
- 1 tbsp scallions, chopped
- 1 tbsp sesame seeds
- 1/2 avocado, diced (optional)

Instructions:

1. In a bowl, combine tuna, soy sauce, sesame oil, rice vinegar, and grated ginger.
2. Gently fold in scallions, sesame seeds, and avocado (if using).
3. Serve immediately with crackers or on a bed of greens.

Caprese Salad

Ingredients:

- 3 large ripe tomatoes, sliced
- 8 oz fresh mozzarella, sliced
- Fresh basil leaves
- 2 tbsp olive oil
- 1 tbsp balsamic vinegar
- Salt and pepper to taste

Instructions:

1. Arrange alternating slices of tomato, mozzarella, and basil on a platter.
2. Drizzle with olive oil and balsamic vinegar.
3. Season with salt and pepper, and serve immediately.

Grilled Asparagus with Hollandaise

Ingredients:

- 1 lb asparagus, trimmed
- 2 tbsp olive oil
- Salt and pepper to taste

For the Hollandaise Sauce:

- 3 egg yolks
- 1/2 cup unsalted butter, melted
- 1 tbsp lemon juice
- Salt and cayenne pepper to taste

Instructions:

1. Preheat grill to medium heat.
2. Toss asparagus with olive oil, salt, and pepper. Grill for 5-7 minutes, turning occasionally.
3. For hollandaise: Whisk egg yolks in a bowl. Gradually add melted butter while whisking until smooth.
4. Stir in lemon juice, salt, and cayenne.
5. Drizzle hollandaise over grilled asparagus and serve.

Shrimp Cocktail

Ingredients:

- 1 lb large shrimp, peeled and deveined
- 1 lemon, halved
- 1 bay leaf
- 1 tsp black peppercorns
- 1 cup cocktail sauce

Instructions:

1. Bring a large pot of water to a boil with lemon halves, bay leaf, and peppercorns.
2. Add shrimp and cook for 2-3 minutes until pink and opaque.
3. Drain and chill the shrimp in ice water for 5 minutes.
4. Serve shrimp with cocktail sauce for dipping.

Summer Berry Salad

Ingredients:

- 1 cup strawberries, sliced
- 1 cup blueberries
- 1 cup raspberries
- 1 cup blackberries
- 1/4 cup fresh mint, chopped
- 2 tbsp honey
- 1 tbsp lime juice

Instructions:

1. Combine all berries in a large bowl.
2. Drizzle with honey and lime juice, then toss gently to coat.
3. Garnish with chopped mint and serve.

Seared Scallops

Ingredients:

- 1 lb scallops, patted dry
- 2 tbsp olive oil
- 1 tbsp butter
- Salt and pepper to taste
- 1 tbsp fresh parsley, chopped (for garnish)

Instructions:

1. Heat olive oil in a skillet over high heat.
2. Season scallops with salt and pepper and sear for 2-3 minutes per side until golden brown.
3. Add butter and allow it to melt over the scallops.
4. Garnish with fresh parsley and serve.

Gazpacho

Ingredients:

- 4 tomatoes, chopped
- 1 cucumber, peeled and chopped
- 1 red bell pepper, chopped
- 1 small red onion, chopped
- 2 cloves garlic, minced
- 2 tbsp olive oil
- 1 tbsp red wine vinegar
- 1 cup tomato juice
- Salt and pepper to taste

Instructions:

1. Combine tomatoes, cucumber, bell pepper, onion, and garlic in a blender.
2. Add olive oil, red wine vinegar, and tomato juice, then blend until smooth.
3. Season with salt and pepper, chill for 2 hours, and serve cold.

Lemon Herb Grilled Chicken

Ingredients:

- 4 boneless, skinless chicken breasts
- 2 tbsp olive oil
- 1 tbsp lemon juice
- 2 cloves garlic, minced
- 1 tsp dried oregano
- Salt and pepper to taste

Instructions:

1. Mix olive oil, lemon juice, garlic, oregano, salt, and pepper in a bowl.
2. Coat chicken breasts with marinade and let sit for 30 minutes.
3. Preheat grill to medium-high heat and cook chicken for 6-7 minutes per side until fully cooked.
4. Serve with additional lemon wedges and fresh herbs.

Ceviche

Ingredients:

- 1 lb fresh shrimp or white fish (like snapper), diced
- 1 cup fresh lime juice
- 1/2 cup red onion, finely chopped
- 1/2 cup cilantro, chopped
- 1-2 serrano chilies, minced
- 1 cucumber, diced
- 1 tomato, diced
- Salt and pepper to taste

Instructions:

1. Place the fish or shrimp in a bowl and pour the lime juice over it.
2. Let the mixture sit in the fridge for 1-2 hours until the fish is "cooked" by the acid.
3. Add the onion, cilantro, chilies, cucumber, and tomato.
4. Season with salt and pepper, mix well, and serve chilled with tortilla chips.

Roasted Corn with Chili Butter

Ingredients:

- 4 ears of corn, husked
- 4 tbsp butter, softened
- 1 tbsp chili powder
- 1/2 tsp smoked paprika
- 1/4 tsp cayenne pepper
- Salt and pepper to taste
- Fresh cilantro, chopped (for garnish)

Instructions:

1. Preheat oven to 400°F (200°C).
2. Place corn on a baking sheet and roast for 20-25 minutes, turning halfway through.
3. In a bowl, combine butter, chili powder, paprika, cayenne, salt, and pepper.
4. Once the corn is roasted, brush with chili butter and garnish with chopped cilantro.

Burrata with Prosciutto

Ingredients:

- 1 ball of burrata cheese
- 4 slices prosciutto
- 1 tbsp olive oil
- Fresh basil leaves
- Salt and pepper to taste

Instructions:

1. Arrange prosciutto slices on a serving plate.
2. Place the burrata cheese in the center.
3. Drizzle with olive oil and season with salt and pepper.
4. Garnish with fresh basil leaves and serve immediately with crusty bread.

Watermelon Feta Salad

Ingredients:

- 3 cups watermelon, cubed
- 1 cup feta cheese, crumbled
- 1/4 cup fresh mint, chopped
- 1 tbsp balsamic glaze
- Salt and pepper to taste

Instructions:

1. In a bowl, combine watermelon, feta, and mint.
2. Drizzle with balsamic glaze and season with salt and pepper.
3. Toss gently and serve chilled.

Grilled Lamb Chops

Ingredients:

- 8 lamb chops
- 2 tbsp olive oil
- 2 cloves garlic, minced
- 1 tbsp rosemary, chopped
- 1 tbsp thyme, chopped
- Salt and pepper to taste

Instructions:

1. Preheat grill to medium-high heat.
2. In a bowl, mix olive oil, garlic, rosemary, thyme, salt, and pepper.
3. Brush the lamb chops with the marinade and let them sit for 15-30 minutes.
4. Grill lamb chops for 3-4 minutes per side for medium-rare, or longer for desired doneness.
5. Serve with a side of roasted vegetables or mashed potatoes.

Mahi-Mahi Tacos

Ingredients:

- 2 mahi-mahi fillets
- 1 tbsp olive oil
- 1 tsp chili powder
- 1 tsp cumin
- Salt and pepper to taste
- 8 small corn tortillas
- Shredded cabbage
- Fresh cilantro, chopped
- Lime wedges
- Salsa or avocado (optional)

Instructions:

1. Preheat grill or skillet to medium heat.
2. Season mahi-mahi fillets with olive oil, chili powder, cumin, salt, and pepper.
3. Grill the fish for 4-5 minutes per side until cooked through.
4. Flake the fish into pieces and fill tortillas with the mahi-mahi.
5. Top with shredded cabbage, cilantro, and a squeeze of lime juice.
6. Serve with salsa or avocado, if desired.

Lobster Bisque

Ingredients:

- 2 lobster tails, cooked and chopped
- 1 tbsp butter
- 1 small onion, chopped
- 2 cloves garlic, minced
- 1/2 cup white wine
- 2 cups lobster stock or seafood broth
- 1 cup heavy cream
- 1/4 tsp paprika
- Salt and pepper to taste

Instructions:

1. In a large pot, melt butter over medium heat and sauté onion and garlic until softened.
2. Add white wine and cook until reduced by half.
3. Stir in lobster stock and bring to a simmer for 10 minutes.
4. Add heavy cream and paprika, then simmer for an additional 5 minutes.
5. Add chopped lobster and season with salt and pepper.
6. Blend with an immersion blender or in batches for a smooth texture.
7. Serve hot with a sprinkle of paprika and fresh herbs.

Grilled Octopus

Ingredients:

- 1 lb octopus
- 2 tbsp olive oil
- 1 lemon, juiced
- 2 cloves garlic, minced
- 1 tsp smoked paprika
- Salt and pepper to taste

Instructions:

1. Preheat grill to medium-high heat.
2. Tenderize octopus by boiling it for 45-60 minutes until tender, then drain and let cool.
3. Toss octopus in olive oil, lemon juice, garlic, paprika, salt, and pepper.
4. Grill octopus for 3-4 minutes per side, until slightly charred.
5. Serve with a drizzle of olive oil and lemon wedges.

Heirloom Tomato Salad

Ingredients:

- 3-4 heirloom tomatoes, sliced
- 1/4 cup fresh basil, chopped
- 1 tbsp balsamic vinegar
- 2 tbsp olive oil
- Salt and pepper to taste

Instructions:

1. Arrange tomato slices on a plate and top with fresh basil.
2. Drizzle with balsamic vinegar and olive oil.
3. Season with salt and pepper and serve immediately.

Avocado Toast with Poached Egg

Ingredients:

- 2 slices of whole-grain bread, toasted
- 1 ripe avocado
- 2 eggs
- 1 tbsp vinegar (for poaching)
- Salt and pepper to taste
- Red pepper flakes (optional)

Instructions:

1. Mash the avocado with salt and pepper, then spread evenly over the toasted bread.
2. To poach the eggs: Bring a pot of water and vinegar to a simmer. Crack an egg into a small bowl and gently slide it into the water. Cook for 3-4 minutes, then remove with a slotted spoon.
3. Place poached eggs on top of avocado toast.
4. Season with red pepper flakes (if desired) and serve immediately.

Zucchini Noodles with Pesto

Ingredients:

- 4 medium zucchinis, spiralized
- 1 cup fresh basil
- 1/4 cup pine nuts
- 2 cloves garlic
- 1/2 cup olive oil
- 1/4 cup Parmesan cheese, grated
- Salt and pepper to taste

Instructions:

1. In a food processor, combine basil, pine nuts, garlic, olive oil, Parmesan, salt, and pepper. Blend until smooth.
2. Sauté zucchini noodles in a hot pan with a drizzle of olive oil for 2-3 minutes until tender but still crisp.
3. Toss the zucchini noodles with pesto sauce until evenly coated.
4. Serve immediately, garnished with extra Parmesan if desired.

Grilled Swordfish

Ingredients:

- 2 swordfish steaks
- 2 tbsp olive oil
- 1 lemon, juiced
- 2 cloves garlic, minced
- 1 tbsp fresh parsley, chopped
- Salt and pepper to taste

Instructions:

1. Preheat grill to medium-high heat.
2. In a small bowl, mix olive oil, lemon juice, garlic, parsley, salt, and pepper.
3. Brush the swordfish steaks with the marinade and let them sit for 10 minutes.
4. Grill the swordfish for 4-5 minutes per side until cooked through.
5. Serve with lemon wedges and a sprinkle of fresh parsley.

Peach and Burrata Salad

Ingredients:

- 2 ripe peaches, sliced
- 1 ball of burrata cheese
- 1 tbsp olive oil
- 1 tbsp honey
- Fresh basil leaves
- Salt and pepper to taste

Instructions:

1. Arrange peach slices on a plate.
2. Tear the burrata cheese into pieces and place it over the peaches.
3. Drizzle with olive oil and honey, then season with salt and pepper.
4. Garnish with fresh basil leaves and serve immediately.

Crab Cakes

Ingredients:

- 1 lb fresh crab meat
- 1/4 cup breadcrumbs
- 1/4 cup mayonnaise
- 1 egg
- 1 tbsp Dijon mustard
- 1/2 tsp Old Bay seasoning
- 2 tbsp fresh parsley, chopped
- 2 tbsp vegetable oil for frying

Instructions:

1. In a bowl, combine crab meat, breadcrumbs, mayonnaise, egg, mustard, Old Bay seasoning, and parsley.
2. Form the mixture into small patties.
3. Heat vegetable oil in a skillet over medium heat.
4. Fry the crab cakes for 3-4 minutes per side until golden brown and crispy.
5. Serve with a squeeze of lemon or tartar sauce.

Grilled Peach Salad

Ingredients:

- 2 peaches, halved and pitted
- 4 cups mixed greens
- 1/4 cup goat cheese, crumbled
- 1/4 cup candied pecans
- 2 tbsp balsamic vinegar
- 2 tbsp olive oil
- Salt and pepper to taste

Instructions:

1. Preheat grill to medium-high heat.
2. Grill peach halves for 2-3 minutes per side until grill marks appear.
3. In a bowl, toss mixed greens, goat cheese, and candied pecans.
4. Drizzle with balsamic vinegar and olive oil, and season with salt and pepper.
5. Top the salad with the grilled peaches and serve immediately.

Grilled Veggie Platter

Ingredients:

- 1 zucchini, sliced
- 1 red bell pepper, sliced
- 1 yellow squash, sliced
- 1 red onion, sliced
- 1 eggplant, sliced
- 2 tbsp olive oil
- 1 tsp dried oregano
- Salt and pepper to taste

Instructions:

1. Preheat grill to medium-high heat.
2. Toss vegetables in olive oil, oregano, salt, and pepper.
3. Grill vegetables for 4-5 minutes per side until tender and charred.
4. Serve the grilled veggies on a platter, drizzling with extra olive oil if desired.

Beef Carpaccio

Ingredients:

- 8 oz beef tenderloin, thinly sliced
- 2 tbsp olive oil
- 1 tbsp lemon juice
- Fresh arugula
- Parmesan shavings
- Capers (optional)
- Salt and pepper to taste

Instructions:

1. Arrange the thin slices of beef on a large plate.
2. Drizzle with olive oil and lemon juice.
3. Top with fresh arugula, Parmesan shavings, and capers (optional).
4. Season with salt and pepper and serve immediately.

Tomato Basil Bruschetta

Ingredients:

- 4 ripe tomatoes, diced
- 1/4 cup fresh basil, chopped
- 2 cloves garlic, minced
- 1 tbsp balsamic vinegar
- 1 tbsp olive oil
- 1 loaf of baguette, sliced
- Salt and pepper to taste

Instructions:

1. Preheat oven to 375°F (190°C).
2. Arrange baguette slices on a baking sheet and toast in the oven for 5-7 minutes.
3. In a bowl, combine tomatoes, basil, garlic, balsamic vinegar, olive oil, salt, and pepper.
4. Spoon the tomato mixture onto the toasted baguette slices.
5. Serve immediately as an appetizer or snack.

Smoked Salmon with Cucumber Salad

Ingredients:

- 8 oz smoked salmon
- 1 cucumber, thinly sliced
- 1 tbsp red onion, finely chopped
- 1 tbsp fresh dill, chopped
- 1 tbsp olive oil
- 1 tbsp lemon juice
- Salt and pepper to taste

Instructions:

1. In a bowl, combine cucumber, red onion, dill, olive oil, lemon juice, salt, and pepper.
2. Toss to combine and let sit for 10 minutes.
3. Serve the smoked salmon alongside the cucumber salad for a light, fresh dish.

Grilled Shrimp Skewers

Ingredients:

- 1 lb large shrimp, peeled and deveined
- 2 tbsp olive oil
- 2 tbsp lemon juice
- 2 cloves garlic, minced
- 1 tsp smoked paprika
- Salt and pepper to taste
- Wooden skewers (soaked in water for 30 minutes)

Instructions:

1. Preheat grill to medium-high heat.
2. In a bowl, toss shrimp with olive oil, lemon juice, garlic, paprika, salt, and pepper.
3. Thread shrimp onto skewers.
4. Grill the shrimp for 2-3 minutes per side until pink and cooked through.
5. Serve with lemon wedges and fresh herbs.

Grilled Chicken Caesar Salad

Ingredients:

- 2 chicken breasts
- 4 cups romaine lettuce, chopped
- 1/4 cup Caesar dressing
- 1/4 cup Parmesan cheese, grated
- Croutons
- Olive oil
- Salt and pepper to taste

Instructions:

1. Preheat the grill to medium-high heat.
2. Season chicken breasts with olive oil, salt, and pepper.
3. Grill the chicken for 6-7 minutes per side until fully cooked. Let rest for a few minutes before slicing.
4. In a large bowl, toss the romaine lettuce with Caesar dressing.
5. Top with sliced grilled chicken, grated Parmesan, and croutons.
6. Serve immediately.

Avocado and Shrimp Ceviche

Ingredients:

- 1 lb shrimp, peeled and deveined
- 2 ripe avocados, diced
- 1/2 red onion, finely chopped
- 1 cucumber, diced
- 2 tomatoes, diced
- 1/4 cup cilantro, chopped
- 1 lime, juiced
- Salt and pepper to taste

Instructions:

1. Cook the shrimp in boiling water for 2-3 minutes until pink and cooked through. Drain and chop into bite-sized pieces.
2. In a bowl, combine shrimp, avocado, red onion, cucumber, tomatoes, cilantro, and lime juice.
3. Season with salt and pepper to taste.
4. Serve chilled with tortilla chips or as a salad.

Stuffed Peppers with Quinoa

Ingredients:

- 4 bell peppers, tops cut off and seeds removed
- 1 cup quinoa, cooked
- 1 can black beans, drained and rinsed
- 1/2 cup corn kernels
- 1 tsp cumin
- 1 tsp chili powder
- 1/2 cup shredded cheese (cheddar or Monterey Jack)
- Salt and pepper to taste

Instructions:

1. Preheat the oven to 375°F (190°C).
2. In a bowl, combine cooked quinoa, black beans, corn, cumin, chili powder, salt, and pepper.
3. Stuff each bell pepper with the quinoa mixture and place them in a baking dish.
4. Sprinkle with shredded cheese.
5. Bake for 25-30 minutes until the peppers are tender and the cheese is melted.
6. Serve warm.

Roasted Beet Salad with Goat Cheese

Ingredients:

- 4 medium beets, peeled and cut into cubes
- 2 tbsp olive oil
- Salt and pepper to taste
- 4 cups mixed greens
- 1/4 cup goat cheese, crumbled
- 1/4 cup walnuts, chopped
- Balsamic vinaigrette

Instructions:

1. Preheat the oven to 400°F (200°C).
2. Toss beet cubes in olive oil, salt, and pepper, and spread them on a baking sheet.
3. Roast for 25-30 minutes until tender.
4. In a large bowl, toss mixed greens with roasted beets, goat cheese, and walnuts.
5. Drizzle with balsamic vinaigrette and serve immediately.

Salmon Poke Bowl

Ingredients:

- 2 salmon fillets, diced
- 1 tbsp soy sauce
- 1 tsp sesame oil
- 1 tbsp rice vinegar
- 1/2 cucumber, julienned
- 1/2 avocado, sliced
- 1/4 cup edamame
- 1/4 cup pickled ginger
- 1 cup sushi rice, cooked
- Sesame seeds for garnish

Instructions:

1. In a bowl, toss the diced salmon with soy sauce, sesame oil, and rice vinegar.
2. In bowls, layer cooked sushi rice, seasoned salmon, cucumber, avocado, edamame, and pickled ginger.
3. Garnish with sesame seeds and serve immediately.

Roasted Vegetable Flatbread

Ingredients:

- 1 store-bought or homemade flatbread
- 1 zucchini, sliced
- 1 red bell pepper, sliced
- 1 eggplant, sliced
- 1 tbsp olive oil
- 1/2 tsp thyme
- 1/2 cup ricotta cheese
- 1/4 cup Parmesan cheese, grated
- Salt and pepper to taste

Instructions:

1. Preheat the oven to 400°F (200°C).
2. Toss zucchini, bell pepper, and eggplant in olive oil, thyme, salt, and pepper.
3. Spread the vegetables on a baking sheet and roast for 20 minutes, flipping halfway through.
4. Top the flatbread with ricotta cheese and roasted vegetables.
5. Sprinkle with Parmesan and bake for another 5-7 minutes until the flatbread is crispy.
6. Slice and serve warm.

Lobster Mac and Cheese

Ingredients:

- 1 lb cooked lobster meat, chopped
- 1 lb elbow macaroni, cooked
- 2 tbsp butter
- 2 tbsp flour
- 2 cups milk
- 2 cups cheddar cheese, shredded
- 1/2 cup Parmesan cheese, grated
- Salt and pepper to taste
- 1/4 cup breadcrumbs (optional)

Instructions:

1. In a large pot, melt butter over medium heat.
2. Stir in flour and cook for 1-2 minutes. Slowly whisk in the milk and cook until thickened.
3. Stir in cheddar and Parmesan cheese until melted and smooth.
4. Add cooked macaroni and lobster meat to the sauce, stirring to combine.
5. Season with salt and pepper.
6. If desired, sprinkle breadcrumbs on top and bake at 375°F (190°C) for 10 minutes until golden and crispy.
7. Serve warm.

Grilled Fennel with Lemon

Ingredients:

- 2 fennel bulbs, sliced into 1/2-inch thick wedges
- 2 tbsp olive oil
- 1 lemon, juiced
- Salt and pepper to taste

Instructions:

1. Preheat grill to medium-high heat.
2. Toss fennel wedges with olive oil, lemon juice, salt, and pepper.
3. Grill fennel for 4-5 minutes per side until tender and slightly charred.
4. Serve immediately, drizzled with extra lemon juice if desired.

Grilled Halloumi Cheese

Ingredients:

- 8 oz halloumi cheese, sliced into 1/2-inch thick slices
- 1 tbsp olive oil
- 1 tbsp lemon juice
- Fresh mint leaves (optional)

Instructions:

1. Preheat grill to medium-high heat.
2. Brush halloumi slices with olive oil and lemon juice.
3. Grill the cheese for 2-3 minutes per side until golden brown and crispy.
4. Garnish with fresh mint leaves and serve warm.

Grilled Fruit Salad

Ingredients:

- 1 pineapple, peeled and cut into wedges
- 2 peaches, halved and pitted
- 1 nectarine, halved and pitted
- 1/2 watermelon, cubed
- 1 tbsp honey
- 1 tbsp lime juice
- Fresh mint leaves for garnish

Instructions:

1. Preheat the grill to medium-high heat.
2. Grill the pineapple, peaches, and nectarine for 2-3 minutes per side until grill marks appear.
3. In a bowl, combine the grilled fruit and watermelon cubes.
4. Drizzle with honey and lime juice, tossing gently to coat.
5. Garnish with fresh mint leaves and serve immediately.

Summer Risotto with Peas

Ingredients:

- 1 cup Arborio rice
- 1 tbsp olive oil
- 1/2 onion, finely chopped
- 2 cloves garlic, minced
- 1/2 cup white wine
- 3 cups vegetable broth, heated
- 1 cup peas (fresh or frozen)
- 1/2 cup Parmesan cheese, grated
- Salt and pepper to taste

Instructions:

1. In a large skillet, heat olive oil over medium heat.
2. Add onion and garlic, cooking until softened, about 3-4 minutes.
3. Stir in Arborio rice and cook for 1-2 minutes.
4. Pour in the white wine, stirring until absorbed.
5. Gradually add heated vegetable broth, one ladle at a time, stirring constantly and letting the liquid absorb before adding more.
6. Once the rice is cooked and creamy (about 18-20 minutes), stir in peas and Parmesan cheese.
7. Season with salt and pepper and serve warm.

Poached Lobster Tail

Ingredients:

- 4 lobster tails
- 4 cups water
- 1 tbsp sea salt
- 1 tbsp lemon juice
- 1 tbsp butter
- Fresh parsley for garnish

Instructions:

1. Bring water to a boil in a large pot.
2. Add sea salt and lemon juice.
3. Using kitchen scissors, cut the top of the lobster shell lengthwise to expose the meat.
4. Lower the lobster tails into the boiling water and poach for 6-8 minutes, until the meat is opaque and tender.
5. Remove lobster tails from the water and brush with melted butter.
6. Garnish with fresh parsley and serve immediately.

Fresh Tuna Sushi

Ingredients:

- 1/2 lb sushi-grade tuna, sliced into 1/4-inch thick pieces
- 1 cup sushi rice, cooked and cooled
- 2 tbsp rice vinegar
- 1 tbsp sugar
- 1 tsp salt
- Soy sauce for dipping
- Wasabi and pickled ginger for garnish

Instructions:

1. In a small bowl, combine rice vinegar, sugar, and salt, stirring until dissolved.
2. Gently mix the vinegar mixture into the cooled sushi rice.
3. Shape a small amount of rice into a mound and top with a slice of tuna.
4. Serve with soy sauce, wasabi, and pickled ginger on the side.

Watermelon Gazpacho

Ingredients:

- 3 cups watermelon, cubed
- 1 cucumber, peeled and chopped
- 1 bell pepper, chopped
- 1/2 red onion, chopped
- 1 clove garlic, minced
- 1/4 cup olive oil
- 2 tbsp red wine vinegar
- Salt and pepper to taste

Instructions:

1. In a blender, combine watermelon, cucumber, bell pepper, onion, and garlic.
2. Blend until smooth, then add olive oil and red wine vinegar.
3. Season with salt and pepper to taste.
4. Chill in the fridge for at least 2 hours before serving.
5. Garnish with additional diced vegetables or herbs if desired.

Seared Ahi Tuna

Ingredients:

- 2 ahi tuna steaks
- 1 tbsp olive oil
- 2 tbsp sesame seeds
- 1 tbsp soy sauce
- 1 tsp wasabi paste (optional)
- Salt and pepper to taste

Instructions:

1. Coat the tuna steaks with olive oil and season with salt and pepper.
2. Roll the tuna in sesame seeds to coat the sides.
3. Heat a skillet over high heat.
4. Sear the tuna for 1-2 minutes on each side for rare, or longer to your preferred doneness.
5. Drizzle with soy sauce and wasabi paste, and serve immediately.

Grilled Eggplant with Feta

Ingredients:

- 2 medium eggplants, sliced into 1/2-inch thick rounds
- 2 tbsp olive oil
- Salt and pepper to taste
- 1/2 cup crumbled feta cheese
- Fresh basil leaves for garnish

Instructions:

1. Preheat the grill to medium-high heat.
2. Brush eggplant slices with olive oil and season with salt and pepper.
3. Grill the eggplant for 4-5 minutes per side until tender and grill marks appear.
4. Sprinkle with crumbled feta cheese and fresh basil before serving.

Summer Squash Frittata

Ingredients:

- 2 zucchini, sliced
- 1 summer squash, sliced
- 8 eggs
- 1/2 cup milk
- 1/4 cup Parmesan cheese, grated
- 1 tbsp olive oil
- Salt and pepper to taste

Instructions:

1. Preheat the oven to 375°F (190°C).
2. In a large skillet, heat olive oil over medium heat.
3. Add the sliced zucchini and summer squash and sauté for 5-7 minutes until tender.
4. In a bowl, whisk together eggs, milk, Parmesan cheese, salt, and pepper.
5. Pour the egg mixture over the vegetables in the skillet.
6. Transfer the skillet to the oven and bake for 15-20 minutes, until the eggs are set.
7. Slice and serve warm.

Grilled Chicken and Peach Salad

Ingredients:

- 2 chicken breasts, grilled and sliced
- 2 peaches, sliced
- 4 cups mixed greens
- 1/4 cup goat cheese, crumbled
- 1/4 cup candied pecans
- Balsamic vinaigrette for dressing

Instructions:

1. Grill the chicken breasts for 6-7 minutes per side, then slice.
2. In a large bowl, combine mixed greens, grilled chicken, sliced peaches, goat cheese, and candied pecans.
3. Drizzle with balsamic vinaigrette and toss gently.
4. Serve immediately.

Shrimp and Grits

Ingredients:

- 1 lb shrimp, peeled and deveined
- 1 cup grits
- 4 cups water
- 1/2 cup cream
- 2 tbsp butter
- 1 tbsp olive oil
- 1/4 tsp paprika
- 1/4 tsp garlic powder
- Salt and pepper to taste

Instructions:

1. Cook the grits in water according to package instructions. Stir in cream, butter, salt, and pepper once done.
2. In a skillet, heat olive oil over medium heat.
3. Add shrimp, paprika, garlic powder, salt, and pepper, and cook for 2-3 minutes until shrimp are pink.
4. Serve the shrimp over a bed of creamy grits.

Roasted Garlic and Herb Mussels

Ingredients:

- 2 lbs mussels, cleaned and debearded
- 4 cloves garlic, minced
- 1/4 cup white wine
- 2 tbsp butter
- 1 tbsp fresh parsley, chopped
- 1 tsp thyme
- Salt and pepper to taste

Instructions:

1. Preheat the oven to 400°F (200°C).
2. In a large skillet, melt butter over medium heat. Add garlic and sauté until fragrant, about 1 minute.
3. Add white wine, thyme, and mussels. Cover and cook for 5-7 minutes, or until the mussels open.
4. Transfer mussels to a baking dish and drizzle with garlic and wine sauce.
5. Roast in the oven for 10-12 minutes.
6. Garnish with parsley, salt, and pepper, and serve warm.

www.ingramcontent.com/pod-product-compliance
Lightning Source LLC
LaVergne TN
LVHW081329060526
838201LV00055B/2534